Purity for the Mind, Body, and Soul

21-Day Purity Fast

by

Assel Jean-Pierre, Jr.

Purity for the Mind, Body, and Soul: 21-Day Purity Fast
Published by Watersprings Publishing, a division of Watersprings Media House, LLC.
P.O. BOX 1284
Olive Branch, MS 38654
www.waterspringsmedia.com
Contact publisher for bulk orders and permission requests.

Copyrights © 2020 by Assel Jean-Pierre Jr.

All rights reserved. No part of this publication may be reproduced, distributed, or transmitted in any form or by any means, including photocopying, recording, or other electronic or mechanical methods, without the prior written permission of the publisher, except in the case of brief quotations embodied in critical reviews and certain other noncommercial uses permitted by copyright law.

Scripture quotations credited to NIV are from the Holy Bible, New International Version. Copyright © 1973, 1978, 1984, 2011 by Biblica, Inc. Used by permission. All rights reserved worldwide.

Scripture quotations marked "ESV" are taken from The Holy Bible, English Standard Version. Copyright © 2000; 2001 by Crossway Bibles, a division of Good News Publishers. Used by permission. All rights reserved.

Printed in the United States of America.

Library of Congress Control Number: 2019919296

ISBN-13: 978-1-948877-41-1

TABLE OF CONTENTS

Introduction 1
Day 1   Identify The Problem 7
Day 2   Identify Your Triggers 10
Day 3   Purity Of The Mind 13
Day 4   Purity Of The Mind Part 2 17
Day 5   Purity Of The Body 21
Day 6   Purity Of Soul 25
Day 7   Bringing It All Together 28
Day 8   Cultivating Purity 32
Day 9   Resist The Devil 35
Day 10   Avoid A False Sense Of Security 38
Day 11   Separation 42
Day 12   Grace 45
Day 13   Prayer 48
Day 14   Fighting The Good Fight 51
Day 15   Claim The Victory 56
Day 16   Terms Of Victory 59
Day 17   Give Thanks 62
Day 18   Share Your Testimony 65
Day 19   It's Not Just About You 69
Day 20   Practice What God Teaches 72
Day 21   Purely The Point 76
          About The Author 81

INTRODUCTION

I'd like to believe I'm a good person, and a good Christian. I've always used the argument that I wasn't too bad, just wasn't perfect. Which you know, because I'm not perfect, gave me a clause to slip up. However, God wasn't satisfied. I was choosing my relationships, choosing how obedient I would be, choosing how obedient I'd allow myself to "accidentally" not be.

God wasn't amused. Especially when He had more for me to do. Especially when He wasn't trying to raise another champion that was living a double-life. Especially when He was trying to build up a David that wouldn't fall to another Bathsheba. So, God allowed me to exercise my free will, and I paid for it. My last relationship was the most draining, most combative, and most exhaustive of my life. It took so much out of me spiritually, mentally, emotionally, and physically. I reached a point in the relationship when I finally said, "Okay, God. You win." The pressure and stress of the relationship alone had me seeking God a lot more than before.

I found myself reading Proverbs, and I began to think to myself, "How did the wisest man in the world fall for something so obvious", he was literally

the wisest man ever. Then God answered me.
He didn't exhibit wisdom in all things.

That's when it hit me. Solomon had 700 wives and over 300 concubines, that definitely is the furthest thing from wisdom. God was showing me, I could be as smart as Solomon or as great as David, but if I didn't overcome the weaknesses in my life, if I wasn't faithful to God in ALL things, then those weaknesses are exactly what the devil would use to destroy me. I couldn't portion off my Christianity anymore or use time delays on when and what I would give Him. It was now, or continue to spiral.

I gave it up right there, in the middle of a relationship where I was already sexually active. I made the decision to be faithful to God in all things, for Him to take complete control and lead my life. I decided to allow God to choose my spouse, and committed to remaining faithful, true, and celibate for Him.

My girlfriend at the time wasn't a fan of the idea, but I wasn't concerned. Shortly thereafter, we broke up. As my walk continued, I was reading the Bible consistently every morning, getting into the habit of consulting God on everything I did. Fasting more than I ever had and studying the word. To be honest, it was truly a great time in my life.

During those times, there was some things God taught me that have not only been a major blessing to me and my marriage, but also to those I've had the opportunity to share them with. Before we get into the fast, I'd like to share these principles with you.

CREATE AN ENVIRONMENT THAT REINFORCES THE LIFESTYLE YOU WANT. SAY "NO" UNAPOLOGETICALLY AND LET GO OF ANYONE WHO ISN'T HELPING.

While my whole life I really did love God and got close to Him, it's the being celibate that really changed my lifestyle. I had to stop hanging around certain family members because they always wanted to chase girls, and I just didn't need that temptation around me. Back then I didn't really try to do anything, but I didn't try not to do anything. I had a "whatever happens, happens" mentality. I had to learn to say no quickly! Literally in those 5 years of celibacy, I was offered sex far more than it was ever offered to me in my life. Telling women that I was celibate and was waiting for marriage made me a target to take down. I had to create a lot of boundaries, and even separate myself from a lot of "friends."

GOD'S PURITY IS A LOT MORE THAN YOU THINK.

We sometimes think the purity God calls us to is simply no sex. God showed me that I shouldn't be engaging in any behavior that would be disrespectful to my wife, if I were married. It's like I was married to God, and I was to remain faithful. So my conversations had to change. I had to avoid being alone with people. No kissing, no touching, no do everything else but "it." Even with TV, social media, all the content I consumed, I became really selective. Not gonna lie, it was TOUGH. Not gonna lie, while I never had intercourse, I had moments when I did slip. I wasn't perfect, but I knew my goal, so whenever I did see myself veer off, I always got back on track. Each slip was a lesson to be learned. An adjustment to be made, until I really got the hang of it.

TAKE CONTROL OF YOUR RELATIONSHIPS.

It wasn't until I mastered this lesson, that I really became okay. I kept thinking, if I told other people my goal, they'd be ok, support me, and leave me alone. However, that was far from the truth. In the beginning when friendships would start, I'd state my stance. They'd say they respected it, and then within a few months of too much talking, too much comfortability, and not enough boundaries, I'd start to veer a little. This happened a few times within my 5 years, and I learned I had to take control. I had to create boundaries, say no, and enforce the no, turn down outings, reject phone calls. I had to be the "bad guy" in order to sustain what God was calling me to do. It was tough, I was so used to not having to do that just letting things flow. However, God was forcing me to learn and master that skill so that I wouldn't have any inappropriate friendships when I was married.

DON'T ENTERTAIN THE ATTENTION.

Once I made my adjustments and learned from my mistakes, I felt like I had things on cruise control. God quickly revealed to me how wrong I was. I realized that even though I wasn't being intimate with anyone, going on dates, or talking late on the phone, I was still entertaining feminine attention, even if it was just a little bit. I would do just enough to keep them interested in me, but not enough to cross any of my boundaries. God called me out and said it straight to me. You don't need their attention. Why are you entertaining it? That was the nail in the coffin for me. From that point on, I lived a life with no holes, no friends that I knew liked me, no texts to old flings waiting for another spark of life, I didn't try to start any new romances. I literally just waited until God revealed to me who my wife was, and what the next move would be. And boy did He!

WE DON'T LOVE PEOPLE FOR WHO OR WHAT THEY ARE, WE LOVE THEM BECAUSE GOD LOVES US.

This by far was one of the most important lessons I learned. It literally taught me how to love. It reshaped how I had been loving everyone in my life. Not just romantically, but with my friends and family as well. It has been the root and definition of how I love. We don't love people based on who they are. People are fickle; they aren't constant. People change. Someone pretty, can one day be not as pretty. Someone kind, can be mean. If we love people for who they are, our love will never be consistent. However, God is always consistent. So if we forgive others because God forgives us, we'll always forgive. Therefore, if we love others because God loves us, we'll always love. It doesn't mean we tolerate abuse, because you must love yourself too. It means the times when your spouse falls short are no justification for you to love them less because you love them based on God's consistency, not on their human inconsistencies. That mindset kept me accountable, and I knew no matter what, whoever God gave me, I'd love them as long as God loved me. Forever IS a LONG TIME.

Little did I know, those experiences and lessons would become the seeds for this book. You picked up this book because you're looking for more in your walk with God. You're looking to take your purity to another level. If you just happened to stumble on this book, maybe God is calling you to another level. Whether it was by intention or not, this fast is about focusing and being intentional about your purity. This isn't about focusing on appearances or what's on the outside (however it is addressed). This book is about doing the heart-work first. To be honest, it was something I had no intentions on writing but God had other plans. God doesn't want partial submission; He doesn't want there to be pieces of you that He doesn't have. It's time to aim for God's standards in ALL aspects of your life.

Thank you for having the courage to take this journey. I pray and know that God will do something special for you during this fast.

PROVERBS 3:5-6 KJV

Trust in the LORD with all thine heart; and lean not unto thine own understanding.
In all thy ways acknowledge him, and he shall direct thy paths.

DAY 1

IDENTIFY THE PROBLEM

Often times, purity has been defined to us primarily in the physical sense. Don't have sex outside of marriage, don't dress a certain way, don't do this and don't do that. However, purity is so much more. True purity is taming and changing your desires, renewing your mind, letting go of unhealthy habits, and walking in righteous and holiness like the texts says. This fast is to clearly define and allow God to show us clearly what purity is, and have it take proper place in our lives. It is to identify any media, content, friends, family, partners, habits, ideals, paradigms, and beliefs that would compromise the character that God calls us to. So that they can be exposed and corrected, whether done alone or done in a community of believers.

So day one is to pray a prayer of clarity and revelation. Ask God to reveal to you all the things that may be slowly keeping you from having the purity He expects. Write them down, make a list, listing all the things, people, places, shows, anything that comes to mind.

These could be things like:
- Forms of social media and the people you follow or look at
- An old ex
- "Friends with benefits"
- Your current boyfriend/girlfriend
- A friend who always makes crude jokes
- Sexual and vulgar music
- A show that exhibits a lot of sexual themes and scenes

Save this list and continue to add to it as God speaks to you. This list is your to-do list. It shows you clearly know what is working against you. In order to defeat your enemy, you must first know your enemy. Once we handle that, the next step is to know ourselves, our triggers, our limits, and our struggles. But first things first.

Meditate on Ephesians 4:22-27. God wants us to let go of our old self, to release the corruption. To renew our minds, our spirits, and walk anew.

Let each prayer be focused on exposing whatever holes the devil may be attacking and ask God to show you what in your mind needs to be renewed and how to go about doing it.

Let's first identify the problem.

In Jesus' name, Amen.

God Bless.

Ephesians 4:22-27 ESV

to put off your old self, which belongs to your former manner of life and is corrupt through deceitful desires, and to be renewed in the spirit of your minds, and to put on the new self, created after the likeness of God in true righteousness and holiness.
Therefore, having put away falsehood, let each one of you speak the truth with his neighbor, for we are members one of another. Be angry and do not sin; do not let the sun go down on your anger, and give no opportunity to the devil.

Jeremiah 33:3 ESV

Call to me and I will answer you and will tell you great and hidden things that you have not known.

DAY 2

IDENTIFY YOUR TRIGGERS

Now that God is beginning to reveal to you the things that compromise your purity, it's important to know why these things have an effect on you. For example, many people who suffer addictions, tend to have undergone a traumatic separation in their youth, so they search for that satisfaction (dopamine highs) and that closeness, in their addictions. Unfortunately, these substitutions usually tend to be self-destructive.

Why is it you have failed relationship after failed relationship? Why is it you entertain people who you know you struggle to say no to? Why do you go on social media and allow your eyes to stare at people who aren't your spouse for unaccounted amounts of time?

In order to overcome the problem, you must identify the problem. That was day one.

Now, you must identify what's pulling you to the very thing God is calling you to leave. Is it trauma? Loneliness? Boredom? Rejection? When you know what the trigger is, you can not only deal with the symptoms, but also deal with the root issue itself. Once the root is dealt with, the symptoms become much easier to handle because you're not fighting against yourself anymore. You stop being your own worst enemy and become your greatest ally.

Like Proverbs 4:23 says, you must guard your heart, because all of your actions stem from your heart. We are all flawed human beings. We all fall short, as it is declared in 1 John 1:8. If we claim we don't have sin in us, we're lying, and there's no truth in us. If you try to believe you can handle it on your own, the Bible says you're foolish. Proverbs 28:26 says those who trust in themselves are fools, so we must walk in wisdom in order to be safe. When we walk in wisdom, we realize we have to replace our vices and our temptations with healthy habits and hobbies to fill the time we were misusing. If we don't, we'll fall back into our vices even worse than before. Luke 11:24-26 confirms this by mentioning the spirit who leaves someone but then returns with 7 stronger spirits.

So today, during your prayer, ask God to reveal what the source of your vices are. What pushes you to do the things that lead you away from God and His will for you? God will reveal it to you, and then show you how to overcome. Sometimes it requires therapy, sometimes it requires prayer, sometimes it requires an intervention, sometimes it's as simple as deleting a number or an app. Let God lead you to do what it takes. Don't hesitate.

In Jesus' name, Amen.

God Bless.

1 John 1:8 NIV

If we claim to be without sin, we deceive ourselves and the truth is not in us.

Proverbs 4:23 NIV

Above all else, guard your heart, for everything you do flows from it.

Proverbs 28:26 NIV

Those who trust in themselves are fools, but those who walk in wisdom are kept safe.

Luke 11:24-26 ESV

When the unclean spirit has gone out of a person, it passes through waterless places seeking rest, and finding none it says, 'I will return to my house from which I came.' And when it comes, it finds the house swept and put in order. Then it goes and brings seven other spirits more evil than itself, and they enter and dwell there. And the last state of that person is worse than the first.

DAY 3

PURITY OF THE MIND

By now, God has begun to show you what to stay away from, and possibly give up forever, during these 21 days. He's begun to speak to your heart and reveal to you why you were even drawn to these things in the first place. We're getting a clearer and clearer picture of the problem. Let's start to identify what our goal is. What actually is purity? Since we as human beings are mind, body, and soul, we should approach our purity the same way. Therefore, on Day 3, we'll focus on purity of the mind.

PROVERBS 4:23 NIV

Above all else, guard your heart, for everything you do flows from it.

Romans 8:5-11 ESV

For those who live according to the flesh set their minds on the things of the flesh, but those who live according to the Spirit set their minds on the things of the Spirit. For to set the mind on the flesh is death, but to set the mind on the Spirit is life and peace. For the mind that is set on the flesh is hostile to God, for it does not submit to God's law; indeed, it cannot. Those who are in the flesh cannot please God.

You, however, are not in the flesh but in the Spirit, if in fact the Spirit of God dwells in you. Anyone who does not have the Spirit of Christ does not belong to Him. But if Christ is in you, although the body is dead because of sin, the Spirit is life because of righteousness. If the Spirit of Him who raised Jesus from the dead dwells in you, He who raised Christ Jesus from the dead will also give life to your mortal bodies through His Spirit who dwells in you.

All that we do starts from our mind. The inner controls the outer. Our bodies are simply vessels that are led by our thoughts, urges, and desires. Even the things we do automatically are simply things we have intentionally or unintentionally trained ourselves to do. There was a point in our life where walking required focus, but now we've done it so much, we can do it without thinking. How many more things are we doing in our lives today without thinking? How many of them are productive? How many times do you just randomly pick up your phone to scroll on social media and waste 5 minutes here, 5 minutes there? How often do you let your thoughts wander about someone, something, or certain times in your life? Christ calls us to be intentional with our thoughts.

2 Corinthians 10: 3-6 ESV says:

For though we walk in the flesh, we are not waging war according to the flesh. For the weapons of our warfare are not of the flesh but have divine power to destroy strongholds. We destroy arguments and every lofty opinion raised against the knowledge of God, and take every thought captive to obey Christ, being ready to punish every disobedience, when your obedience is complete.

Even Christ set the standard for us when He said, if you even LUST after a woman, it is considered adultery. So purity of the mind, is something Christ emphasized.

When your mind is pure, you're not constantly viewing normal things in a sexual way. Have you ever played the word game where some letters are missing, and you fill in the rest? S _ x ? For someone who's constantly thinking about music, the first thing that comes to mind might be S-a-x, a saxophone, but for someone always thinking about raunchy things, they'll probably see S-e-x. So our mind is shaping everything we see and every interaction we have. So we're either sexualizing everything, or seeing things as they are.

When your mind is pure:
- You're not constantly telling dirty jokes
- You're not trying to shift every conversation to a sexual topic
- You're not constantly trying to sexualize the people around you

These are just a few examples. Remember your mind only expresses what you feed it. That's why purity is mind, body, AND soul. During this fast, feed your mind purity daily. Avoid sexual jokes, innuendos, conversations, flirting, etc. (outside the context of marriage.)

If your mind is dirty, let's start cleaning it up.

Our prayer today should be focused on God purifying and renewing our mind. To help us take any thoughts that aren't pleasing to Him into captivity. Ask God to continue to bring light to where your mind is weakest. Implore the Holy Spirit to be the leader of your thoughts, and to always subdue the flesh. Ask God to guide your daily interactions in a way that you're building your purity, instead of slowly chipping away at it. Surrender your heart and mind to Christ, and He'll get your mind right.

In Jesus' name, Amen.

God Bless.

DAY 4

PURITY OF THE MIND PART 2

In continuation with pursuing purity of the mind, let's identify how the mind is shaped.

Our mindsets, how we perceive information, how we view the world, are created either by firsthand experience or by secondhand knowledge. People share things with us, and we choose to believe it as fact, or we experience things and accept it as fact. Our mindsets or our paradigms determine how we approach everything in life.

If we have a growth paradigm, we're open to trying new things, tackling different endeavors, or even stepping out of our comfort zone. However, if we have a negative paradigm, we never want to do anything, because we feel like it won't ever turn out good.

Mindsets continue to shape themselves by repeated behavior or experience. If every time you practice you get better, you'll believe more and more that practice makes perfect. However, if no matter how much you practice, you see no improvement, you'll be discouraged from putting effort into things because no matter how hard you try, it won't work out.

How we were raised, the things around us, our family, friends, and community, also shape us in ways we may not be willing to acknowledge. Behavioral scientists tend to agree that nature (your genes, bloodline) and nurture (culture, people, environment) have a strong impact on who we are. Well how does this factor into purity?

If you want to change something, it helps to best understand how it works. When you realize that your mind is built by your environment, your genes, and your circle of family and friends, then you now know where to start if you want to change your mindset. That's why the Bible says in Philippians 4:8 to think about what is true, honorable, pure, holy, excellent. The more we think of these things, the more we feed our mind these values and principles, the more they shape our mind, and in turn shape our character.

When couples want to set the mood, they play romantic music, dim the lights, and set the ambience. Well, if you want to truly start to purify your mind, you're going to have to start setting the mood. That means taking all you do into account.

The music you listen to, should express ideas and messages that agree with the lifestyle you're pursuing.

When you see people who are dressed provocatively, you have to train yourself to bounce your eyes, and not gaze upon them. Whether this be in person or through social media.

Your circle of friends should be people who are leading you closer to Christ and the characteristics He embodies.

Your timeline on social media should be accounts

and messages that are constantly pushing beliefs, ideals, and mindsets that you want to have. If you're aiming for purity, it can be challenged if you're following accounts that are constantly posting provocative content. Instead, replace your timeline with edifying content, that will slowly shape your paradigm into one that aligns with your values.

Remember, the brain can be trained, either intentionally or unintentionally. So while we may have some bad habits, it's never too late to create good habits. Take inventory of all the influences in your life, direct or indirect. Ask yourself, "Is this promoting the lifestyle that God is leading me to?" Make changes as God leads you. Always remember we're affected by everything, whether it be a little or a lot, whether we acknowledge it or not. It's important that you take what goes into your mind very seriously.

As they say, "A mind is a terrible thing to waste."

Luke 6:45 ESV

The good person out of the good treasure of his heart produces good, and the evil person out of his evil treasure produces evil, for out of the abundance of the heart his mouth speaks.

Philippians 4:8 ESV

Finally, brothers, whatever is true, whatever is honorable, whatever is just, whatever is pure, whatever is lovely, whatever is commendable, if there is any excellence, if there is anything worthy of praise, think about these things.

Today's prayer is to ask God to help us undo the bad habits, paradigms, and beliefs we've picked up throughout life. Ask the Holy Spirit to transform and renew your mind, to allow you to see things the way He would like you to see them. Ask God to help you see like Christ, instead of seeing like man. Pray for the strength to break bad habits and beliefs, no matter how difficult it may be. Pray for an environment of God-sent people that will support you in this journey. God will guide you every step of the way if you're willing and faithful. Start today. It's about time you made up your mind.

In Jesus' name, Amen.

God Bless.

DAY 5
PURITY OF THE BODY

1 Thessalonians 4:3-5 ESV

For this is the will of God, your sanctification that you abstain from sexual immorality; that each one of you know how to control his own body in holiness and honor, not in the passion of lust like the Gentiles who do not know God;

Romans 8:13 ESV

For if you live according to the flesh you will die, but if by the Spirit you put to death the deeds of the body, you will live.

1 Corinthians 6:12-20 ESV

"All things are lawful for me," but not all things are helpful. "All things are lawful for me," but I will not be dominated by anything. "Food is meant for the stomach and the stomach for food"— and God will destroy both one and the other. The body is not meant for sexual immorality, but for the Lord, and the Lord for the body. And God raised the Lord and will also raise us up by his power. Do you not know that your bodies are members of Christ? Shall I then take the members of Christ and make them members of a prostitute? Never! Or do you not know that he who is joined to a prostitute becomes one body with her? For, as it is written, "The two will become one flesh." But he who is joined to the

> Lord becomes one spirit with him. Flee from sexual immorality. Every other sin a person commits is outside the body, but the sexually immoral person sins against his own body. Or do you not know that your body is a temple of the Holy Spirit within you, whom you have from God? You are not your own, for you were bought with a price. So glorify God in your body.

Now that we've established purity of the mind, let's define purity of the body. God calls us to not only abstain from sexual immorality, but to also control our body in holiness and honor. The body wasn't meant for sexual immorality. That means God did not design us to have multiple sexual partners. We were designed by God to have only one, our spouse.

Though we see examples of biblical characters who had multiple wives (David, Solomon, Jacob), there was never any benefit that came from it, and it usually led to turmoil. When Abraham slept with Hagar, that actually ended up creating more problems for him, short-term and long-term. The human body is designed so that when you're intimate with someone, your body will "crave" them more and more, and your affections for that person grow. When this is done in the context of marriage, it works beautifully. Outside of marriage is where issues arise.

However, purity of the body isn't limited to only sexual intercourse. We must train ourselves to hold sacred what is meant for our spouse and our spouse alone. Make-out sessions, petting, mutual rubbing, these are some of the many things that have created many blurred lines among what is allowed, and what isn't. So we now have a culture of Christians that try and do everything they can, without doing "it." The problem with that is, lust is never satisfied; it always wants more. So as we continue to test our boundaries, we continue to go further and further until we cross lines we initially had no intentions of crossing.

How do we avoid that? Train yourself to be faithful to your spouse now. Whether you know who your future spouse is, practice being faithful to him or her right now. Don't participate in any intimate behavior with anyone who's not your spouse. This practice may seem radical, but it is beneficial. If you can be faithful to someone you're not even with, how much more can you be faithful when you and your spouse are together?

Remember, though popular culture says your body is your own, and you can do whatever you want, the Bible says quite the opposite. 1 Corinthians 6:19-20 says, "Our body is a temple of the Holy Spirit within us, we are not our own, we were bought at a price. Our bodies belong to God, and we are to honor him with them."

So during this fast and after, let your daily goal be to honor God with your body. To not compromise or cave into the desires of the flesh, but to stand firm. While the world says do whatever you want with your body, followers of Christ submit their bodies to Him.

Let your prayer today be that you not only abstain from sexual immorality, but you truly cherish your body the way God sees fit. Pray that you take care of your temple and honor God with it. Pray that the urges of the flesh don't lead you astray, and that you are given the strength to resist. Rededicate yourself to God; mind, body, and soul. Let us find life in the Spirit and put to death the deeds of the body. With our mind right, now we can get our body right.

In Jesus' name, Amen.

God Bless.

DAY 6

PURITY OF SOUL

Galatians 5:16-26 ESV

But I say, walk by the Spirit, and you will not gratify the desires of the flesh. For the desires of the flesh are against the Spirit, and the desires of the Spirit are against the flesh, for these are opposed to each other, to keep you from doing the things you want to do. But if you are led by the Spirit, you are not under the law. Now the works of the flesh are evident: sexual immorality, impurity, sensuality, idolatry, sorcery, enmity, strife, jealousy, fits of anger, rivalries, dissensions, divisions, envy, drunkenness, orgies, and things like these.
I warn you, as I warned you before, that those who do such things will not inherit the kingdom of God. But the fruit of the Spirit is love, joy, peace, patience, kindness, goodness, faithfulness, gentleness, self-control; against such things there is no law. And those who belong to Christ Jesus have crucified the flesh with its passions and desires.
If we live by the Spirit, let us also keep in step with the Spirit. Let us not become conceited, provoking one another, envying one another.

We've learned about purity of the mind and how everything starts there. We've discussed purity of the body and understand that our bodies are not our own, and that we are to honor God with them. Now let's tackle the last aspect: purity of the soul.

Your soul determines where your heart and desires lie. Who is your god? Is it the Creator of the universe? Jehovah, Yahweh, Jesus Christ? Or is it yourself? Is it Satan? Is it Money? Pleasure? Work?

Matthew 6:21 ESV says, "For where your treasure is, there your heart will be also."

Whatever is your god will dictate your values, your sacrifices, your worship, and also your desires. Our mind is our reasoning, our deduction of the world. Our body is the vessel used to carry out what we set ourselves to do. Our soul is what determines if any of this is right or wrong. The soul is considered the heart of who man is, our inner core, while the mind is our thoughts and consciousness. To put it simply, our desires come from our souls (i.e. love, attention, companionship, etc.), while our minds decide how to satisfy those desires (God, pleasure, money, etc.)

When God is number one in your life, your desires become His desires. Psalm 37:4 Delight yourself in the LORD, and he will give you the desires of your heart. When you find joy in God, and submit your heart to Him, you start to want what He wants for you. For example, you'll actually want to cultivate purity in a world that only wants to cultivate lust. Anything else that you put above God will only cause you to be empty inside. Money won't satisfy, pleasure will get stale; that longing in your soul, it's only a void God can fill.

Purity For The Mind, Body, And Soul

So achieving purity of the soul is taking inventory of your life and making sure each thing is in its rightful place. Money isn't evil, the love of it is. Pleasure isn't a bad thing, just too much of it is. You have to make sure God is the number one thing in your life, and that everything else in your life falls under Him. When God is the utmost priority in your life, your life will bear the fruits. You won't engage in sexual immorality, impurity, fits of anger, or dissensions. You will show love, joy, peace, and patience. Let God create in you a clean heart and renew a right spirit within you.

Our prayer today:
Father God, my heart, my mind, my soul belongs to You. If I've put anything above You Lord, show me. Show me how to put You back on top and keep You there. I surrender myself to You Lord, and I ask You to lead me and guide me in Your will for me. I let go of anything that's causing me to falter in my walk with You. I thank You for bringing me this far and loving me despite who I am. I thank You for continuing to walk with me and loving me into who I will be. You are number one in my life, and I want it to stay that way forever. Help me keep that promise, even as the enemy tries to prevent that. I thank You, Lord, for already giving me the victory.

In Jesus' name, Amen.

God Bless.

DAY 7

BRINGING IT ALL TOGETHER: BODY MIND & SOUL

1 THESSALONIANS 5:23 ESV

Now may the God of peace himself sanctify you completely and may your whole spirit and soul and body be kept blameless at the coming of our Lord Jesus Christ.

We've spent all of week one identifying the problems. We asked God to show us where in our lives are we doing things that compromise our purity. We asked God to reveal to us the triggers that keep us coming back to these behaviors. We've identified purity of the mind, the body, and the soul. Today, we're bringing it all together.

We as human beings function best when we are in sync: mind, body, and soul. We're layered, and each layer is just as important as the other. If your body is well kept, but your mind is a wreck, you're lacking. If your mind is sharp, but your soul craves all things carnal, you'll always find smart ways to do the wrong thing. We must be balanced in all aspects of our lives to truly maximize God's calling in our lives. 1 Thessalonians 5:23 says when God sanctifies us, it will be completely, not partially. Our Spirit (mind), soul, and body need to be consistently preserved and held blameless until Christ's return. It's not saying that if we mess up, we'll lose salvation, for all have fallen short. The verse is making it clear that purity should be our goal in ALL aspects of our lives, each and every day.

When you have time, meditate on not just the verse but the entire chapter. It lists many important action steps, that reflect the true character of Christ.

Purity is the total package. If you read the Bible every day, but entertain sexual content, themes, or shows, you're compromising yourself. If you don't engage in physical intimacy with anyone, yet you entertain thoughts about them, you're compromising your purity. Your thoughts, your actions, and your heart have to all be aligned. When they are, it makes this battle, and yes it's a battle, easier. You can't pick and choose when you want to be pure, because now you're opening up avenues where the Devil can attack. Remember, he's a prowling lion, seeking whom he can devour. Any opening we give him, any weakness we show, he will gladly take advantage of it. Once these weaknesses are attacked, the goal is to spread and ruin other aspects of our life, so that small issues, if not handled, can lead to much larger ones. So in order for us not to be led to ruin, we actually should make a big deal about our little weaknesses. It's the little things that lead to the bigger things. That can work in the positive, but it also works in the negative. That's why the songs says, "O be careful little eyes what you see, little ears what you hear, little hands what you do, and little feet where you go."

Purity is no little task, but it is made up of small actions that lead to a big result. Proverbs 3:6 says, "In all your ways acknowledge him, and he will make straight your paths." We've identified, and defined purity in all aspects. So today, let's bring it all together.

*Our prayer for today is that we ask God to help us be pure in all aspects of our lives. To take all that we've learned this week, to create a major transformation in us, not just in how we act, but in how we think, and how we live. Pray that God be the guiding light in each facet of your life.
To give you the strength to let go of the things you're struggling to let go of. To renew your mind, body, and soul for Him. Acknowledge God in all your ways; your thoughts, your plans, and your decisions. Submit them all to Him, and thankHim for directing your path.
Thank God for each daily victory and grace for the days you fall short. Ask Him to surround you with people who will draw you closer to His character, and not further away. Thank Him for the work He's doing in you, and focus on just how much more He wants to grow with you.*

In Jesus' name, Amen.

God Bless.

DAY 8

CULTIVATING PURITY

2 PETER 1:5-8 ESV

For this very reason, make every effort to supplement your faith with virtue, and virtue with knowledge, and knowledge with self-control, and self-control with steadfastness, and steadfastness with godliness, and godliness with brotherly affection, and brotherly affection with love. For if these qualities are yours and are increasing, they keep you from being ineffective or unfruitful in the knowledge of our Lord Jesus Christ.

Now that we've identified the problem, we need to work on replacing the old behavior with the new. 2 Peter 1:5-8 is a great place to start. In our walk with God, it all starts with faith; belief that God is who He says He is and that Jesus is God's Son. This is what aligns our hearts with God. So in order to support that faith, to keep it strong, we must support it with virtue. Virtue is defined as "behavior showing high moral standards." We know that all morals come from God, so we can define virtue as "Behavior showing Christ-like standards." Our faith is made stronger when we act like Christ. However, Peter doesn't stop there. With our faith, with our Christ-like character, we must add knowledge. Knowledge could be scripture reading and knowing the word, studying apologetics, or being like the Bereans. From knowledge, we must exhibit self-control, the ability to discipline ourselves. Why? Because our faith, our virtue, what we know, will be tested; it will be challenged. If we're not able to resist the devil, he won't flee. That's why self-control, is followed by steadfastness. Don't give in; don't stop resisting.

The verse continues, add godliness to your steadfastness. Godliness is defined as "conforming to the laws and wishes of God." So as we resist, we must align our desires, our wants, all our ways to what God wants for us. Godliness then leads to brotherly love. I think God puts this towards the end because He wants to make sure throughout our pursuit of Christ-like character, we don't forget His commandment. Love your neighbor as yourself. Throughout our journey, we can't get so holy that we become comfortable disrespecting our neighbor. God calls us to love. Which is the last quality? Love. Love can only come through having a relationship with God. When we follow these steps, our walk with Christ will not only allow us to continue to grow, but be effective and fruitful in Jesus name.

These are the qualities we must replace with the things we've been fasting from. So if you unfollowed accounts that posted raunchy content, replace it with accounts that promote these values. If you stopped talking to friends who were always leading you to compromise your boundaries, surround yourself with people who will help you uphold your boundaries and lead you towards Christ. Your environment, and your circle of friends have a major impact on you. Each thing you've stopped or have been fasting from, replace it with the qualities and character you want to exhibit.

Let us all take heed so that we may be effective and fruitful in the knowledge of our Lord Jesus Christ.

As you pray today, ask God to show you who you should allow in your life and what you should allow in your life. Pray that He gives you the discernment to be able to see through the people that are already in your life. Ask God to help you develop virtue, knowledge, self-control, steadfastness, godliness, brotherly affection, and most importantly, love.

In Jesus' name, Amen.

God Bless.

Purity For The Mind, Body, And Soul

DAY 9

RESIST THE DEVIL

LUKE 11:24-26 ESV

"When the unclean spirit has gone out of a person, it passes through waterless places seeking rest, and finding none it says, 'I will return to my house from which I came.' And when it comes, it finds the house swept and put in order. Then it goes and brings seven other spirits more evil than itself, and they enter and dwell there. And the last state of that person is worse than the first."

It's been eight days now. You're now experiencing the results of the fast. You have more free time. You've become more perceptive and intentional about what you watch, who you talk to, and what you talk about. It's not completely automatic, but it's starting to be. But there's another drawback. With all this free time, sometimes it becomes idle time. Your old habits are starting to stir, wondering why they haven't been carried out these last couple days. People you stopped talking to are beginning to notice your absence. Part of you is starting to miss the attention from the people you cut off. These old habits won't die easy.

This moment during the fast is a pivotal one. It's when the devil starts pushing back to see if you'll actually stand firm with your commitments. Remember, Luke 11:24-26 talks about a spirit that leaves a man, but when it can't find a place to rest, it comes back with seven times more evil. So much so, that if it does enter in, it's going to be much worse than it was before. If we're not at that moment, we're nearing that moment. Those bad habits, bad influences, the things that were compromising your purity, they want to come back. They want to reenter your life stronger than before.

This is when you must resist more than ever. Take it moment by moment, day by day. Just win the day. Don't give in, maintain your fast, maintain the cultivation of your purity. Dive into the activities you have chosen to replace the bad habits even more. That will help you deal with the pushback. Remember, resist the devil and he will flee. So now that he's pushing, it's now time that we resist. And we don't stop resisting until he flees. When he flees, we get stronger and prepare for the next attack.

You're getting stronger. The prayers you're praying, God hears you. Don't give up. Don't give in.

Purity For The Mind, Body, And Soul

Our prayer for today is for God to give us the strength to resist. To grant us the endurance so we don't give up. To hold us and fight for us when we feel like we can't go any longer. To lift us up and carry us when we feel like we're worn out. To take full control of our battles and guide us through. Thank Him for carrying you through and thank Him for the victory.

In Jesus' name, Amen.

God Bless.

DAY 10

AVOID A FALSE SENSE OF SECURITY

MATTHEW 26:41 NIV

"Watch and pray so that you will not fall into temptation. The spirit is willing, but the flesh is weak."

1 PETER 5:8 ESV

Be sober-minded; be watchful. Your adversary the devil prowls around like a roaring lion, seeking someone to devour.

As you're growing during this fast, don't allow yourself to get comfortable. Don't allow yourself to ease up on your boundaries. The moment you relax, that's the moment the devil will attack. When we look back to David and the situation with Bathsheba, David was caught in a moment of fatigue. The chapters prior tell of two wars David was involved in, and when he was supposed to go back out with his army, he decided to stay in the city. Feeling fatigued, feeling weary, his decision making was weak. So when he saw Bathsheba, it was easy for him to be led by the flesh because his spirit was weary.

Always keep in mind, the devil is prowling. He doesn't take days off. You resist, he flees, but not too far, he just tries another approach, another angle. That's why we must guard our hearts, and approach purity as an all-encompassing effort. If you leave just one weakness unguarded, rest assured that's where the devil will attack. Throughout the Bible, he's made a habit of attacking our weakest points when we're feeling the weakest. Even Jesus had to deal with it. When Satan came to tempt him, Jesus had been in the wilderness fasting for 40 days. People have attempted this fast, and many if not all have died, no one has made it to 40 days. So it's when Christ was weary and weak, that the devil came to tempt Him. First with food, then with testing His Father's love, and then with glory, power, and adulation. Yet Christ stood firm. Why? Because He never let His guard down. Lack of food didn't alter His character, lack of comfort didn't alter His character, loneliness didn't alter His character. Instead, He was rooted in scripture, so when the devil attacked, He allowed God to be strong for Him.

Purity is not an event. It's a process, a process that will be constantly tested. We must resist, but we also must get stronger and stronger. Spend time in the word. Start creating a list of scriptures that you can turn to when times get challenging. They will hold you when you're feeling weak.

Some scriptures I use to strengthen me are:

Psalm 101:3-4 ESV

I will not set before my eyes anything that is worthless. I hate the work of those who fall away; it shall not cling to me. A perverse heart shall be far from me; I will know nothing of evil.

Psalm 119:37 ESV

Turn my eyes from looking at worthless things; and give me life in your ways

Job 31:1 ESV

"I have made a covenant with my eyes; how then could I gaze at a virgin?

Create your own list. Build up your defenses on God, not on your own merits. Don't get comfortable, and don't grow weary in well-doing. Stay vigilant, the devil doesn't take breaks and neither should you!

Your prayer today will be focused on asking God to continue to fight on your behalf. To protect you from yourself, when you're being tempted. To lead you to the verses and scriptures that will strengthen you and keep you during your moments of weakness. Ask God to help you continue to strengthen your walk with Him. Continue to invite Him into every aspect of your life, to teach you true submission to His will. Ask Him to hold you together when you can barely hold yourself together. He will come through for you. Always.

In Jesus' name, Amen.

God Bless.

DAY 11

SEPARATION

1 CORINTHIANS 6:15-17 ESV

Do you not know that your bodies are members of Christ? Shall I then take the members of Christ and make them members of a prostitute? Never! Or do you not know that he who is joined to a prostitute becomes one body with her? For, as it is written, "The two will become one flesh." But he who is joined to the Lord becomes one spirit with him.

Today, we look into not only fasting from certain activities that compromise our purity, but complete separation. Remember, the Bible tells us to flee sexual immorality, to leave youthful passions, to avoid anything that isn't righteous in God's eyes. The goal of our fast isn't to just take a break from these activities and then return to them. It's to eliminate them completely.

The more we entertain sexual immorality, lustful images, carnal mindsets, vulgar content, and sexual themes, the more they cleave to us. Like 1

Corinthians 6:15-17 says, when you join together with the ungodly, the flesh becomes one. That's not limited to just physical connections. The Bible doesn't clearly speak of the term "soul ties," but it does make it clear that laying with the enemy will create a connection. To move forward, we have to sever those connections. That means severing the mediums of those connections. If it's a person, we're deleting numbers, blocking contacts, and ending all contact. If it's shows, we're simply not allowing ourselves to continue watching them. If it's sexual content, we're placing safeguards on our devices, getting accountability partners, and removing all inappropriate content. Whatever or whomever it is, the separation needs to be complete, sudden, and swift.

Ephesians 5:3 says, "There shouldn't even be a hint of sexual immorality, impurity, or greed among God's people. Not even a hint." Yesterday, we talked about how the devil is searching for any openings or any hints of weakness he can find. That means it's our responsibility to take care of our weaknesses. If you don't want to do something, don't put yourself in an environment where it can happen. If you know every time you're alone with this person, you'll compromise yourself, then stop putting yourself in that situation. Put a stop to it and create clear standards and boundaries. If we continue to be vague about our standards of purity and boundaries, then we will always cross the line, primarily because there was never a real line to begin with. You must be firm and bring every thought into submission that isn't of God. Hold yourself accountable, create clear and firm boundaries based on God's standards, not your own. Take action now on creating the separation necessary. You already know what or who has to go. God has already put it on your heart, you're just stalling. You don't have the luxury of time. If God is impressing on your heart to remove it, it's because it has to go now, not when it's convenient or when you feel emotionally ready. Now's the time to move forward.

God can't fight your battles if you're sleeping with the enemy. Create separation, and then make it permanent.

Our prayer today is to ask God to help us be obedient to His instructions for our lives. To have the courage to cut what He says to cut, to leave what He says to leave, and to never go back or look back.
Lord, help us with the people and things that have a hold on us. In the name of Jesus, grant us victory and freedom from any stronghold. Deliver us in Jesus' name, through the power of His blood. We thank You for the victory. Keep us from going back from what You've already defeated for us. We praise Your name and we love You.

In Jesus' name, Amen.

God Bless.

DAY 12

GRACE

2 Corinthians 12:7-10 ESV

So to keep me from becoming conceited because of the surpassing greatness of the revelations, a thorn was given me in the flesh, a messenger of Satan to harass me, to keep me from becoming conceited. Three times, I pleaded with the Lord about this, that it should leave me. But he said to me, "My grace is sufficient for you, for my power is made perfect in weakness." Therefore, I will boast all the more gladly of my weaknesses, so that the power of Christ may rest upon me. For the sake of Christ, then, I am content with weaknesses, insults, hardships, persecutions, and calamities. For when I am weak, then I am strong.

In our life-long journey of purity, there are moments when we will fall. It may not be as egregious as adultery, or a porn addiction, but if you don't make quick corrections when you do fall, those "small" slips will lead to the "bigger slips." We must keep in mind, when we do fall, we should not fall into a spiral of guilt and shame. That's exactly what the devil wants. He wants you to pull away from God because you've fallen and you're "dirty." However, when we fall, hiding from God (like Adam and Eve), is the absolute last thing we should do. In fact, we should run towards Christ even more. He is the one who will clean us up from our muck.

Paul talks about how he suffered because of a spirit that wouldn't leave him be. He begged and pleaded with God to remove it. Instead, God responded by saying His grace is sufficient, and His power is made perfect in our weakness. Therefore, we should look at our calamities, trials, and tribulations with a fresh perspective. The situations that test our faith, are the ones that strengthen us. When we struggle with bad habits, secret sins, or vices, we grow weak from the constant struggle. However, our weakness is when God is even stronger in our lives. When we're weak, we also have less energy to fight God anymore, so while we're more susceptible to falling, we're also more willing to listen and be obedient. Look at Jonah, in the beginning he refused to do God's will, but after God had him in the mouth of a whale, he surrendered and was willing to be obedient.

Don't beat yourself up when you fall. You're human. Don't make light of it or make it excusable either. When you fall, analyze what happened that led to your fall, make the necessary changes, and move forward towards the path of being better.

Remember, all have sinned and fallen short of the glory of God. God's grace is what allows you to learn from your mistakes, grow, and "sin no more."

No matter your mistakes, your shortcomings, or your weaknesses, His grace is sufficient.

Today, we pray, Lord forgive us of our sins, conscious and unconscious. Forgive us of our shortcomings. When we fall, help us run to You and not from You. Help us to learn from our mistakes and improve so we don't repeat them. Help us to accept Your grace and learn how to forgive ourselves when we don't do what we want to do. We thank You for being our strength when we have no strength left. We are content with the trials and tribulations that come our way because we know all these things are here to make us stronger in You. Thank You, Lord.

In Jesus' name, Amen.

God Bless.

DAY 13

PRAYER

MATTHEW 26:41 ESV

Watch and pray that you may not enter into temptation. The spirit indeed is willing, but the flesh is weak.

1 THESSALONIANS 5:16-18 ESV

Rejoice always, pray without ceasing, give thanks in all circumstances; for this is the will of God in Christ Jesus for you.

We are in a battle with an enemy who does not cease. When we resist him, he flees, but he comes right back. That's why it's of the utmost importance that we stay connected to the Savior. If communication with God is something you take casually, then you will receive casual results. If you take your prayer life seriously, then you will witness and experience serious changes in your life.

Matthew 26:41 tells us, not only to keep our guard up, but to constantly stay in prayer. It's not enough to just watch. There may be things happening that we can't see. For that reason, prayer is key. Through prayer, God will guide you and reveal to you the things you can't see. Through prayer, schemes of the devil, that you had no clue were in motion, are destroyed. Through prayer, you're able to confess your weakness, your fatigue, and call upon God for strength and endurance. Through prayer, God can further reveal things in your environment that aren't good for you.

Prayer is a personal one on one moment between you and God. Yes, corporate prayer is also important. Families should pray together, couples, friends, churches, and even strangers should at times. However, never neglect that one on one time between you and God. Jesus set that example for us. He would pray with others, do miracle after miracle, but many times throughout the Bible He would isolate Himself, and talk with God.

1 Thessalonians 5:16-18 tells us that we should pray without ceasing. The translation isn't saying pray nonstop, it means to pray frequently, pray often. Remember, our spirit is willing, but our flesh is weak. Prayer keeps us connected. It keeps us strong. Prayer fuels us up when we're at our lowest. Throughout the day, we get tired and worn out, our resolve isn't as strong as it was early in the day. That's when the devil attacks; that's when people compromise their standards, when we're tired. The way we fight back, is to stay in constant contact with God. Sometimes your prayer can be conversational, sometimes it can be casual, and other times more serious. Sometimes you're asking for something but sometimes you're thanking Him for what you

already have. When you pray, be truthful, be raw, and be open to God. He's the one person you know won't ever repeat your secrets. He always wants what's best for you.

You can't have purity without prayer.

Even after the fast is over, create and maintain a prayer routine that you follow and keep faithfully. It will change your life.

The prayer for today is for you to just speak to God about whatever is on your heart. Whatever it may be, your joys, your sorrows, your worries. Be sure to be open, be transparent, and let it all out. God hears you, and He will answer.

In Jesus' name, Amen.

God Bless.

DAY 14

FIGHTING THE GOOD FIGHT

ROMANS 8:35-39 ESV

*Who shall separate us from the love of Christ? Shall tribulation, or distress, or persecution, or famine, or nakedness, or danger, or sword? As it is written, "For your sake we are being killed all the day long; we are regarded as sheep to be slaughtered."
No, in all these things we are more than conquerors through him who loved us. For I am sure that neither death nor life, nor angels nor rulers, nor things present nor things to come, nor powers, nor height nor depth, nor anything else in all creation will be able to separate us from the love of God in Christ Jesus our Lord.*

2 CORINTHIANS 10:3-4 ESV

For though we walk in the flesh, we are not waging war according to the flesh. For the weapons of our warfare are not of the flesh but have divine power to destroy strongholds.

2 Chronicles 15:7 NIV

But as for you, be strong and do not give up, for your work will be rewarded."

Psalm 73:26 ESV

My flesh and my heart may fail, but God is the strength of my heart and my portion forever.

Serving God completely is warfare. Having Him as number one in your life is literally an open challenge to the devil. The devil doesn't want to see that because he knows the power of just one person putting God first completely as David, Daniel, Abraham, and Moses. God can use one person to do amazing things and inspire millions. If you're in this fast, it's because He wants to use you. There's something special He has for you. A great work, a calling, but in order to truly be prepared, there are things we not only have to let go, but constantly fight. The last thing the devil wants to see is us succeed. He will never stop trying to attack us. He will never stop aiming for our purity because he knows the flesh is weak. 2 Corinthians 10:4 makes us aware that even though we walk in the flesh, we aren't fighting on fleshly terms. We are fighting on spiritual terms. Whatever fleshly desires you're suffering from, you can't solve them with fleshly solutions. Your loneliness won't be solved by getting a partner, sleeping with someone, or never-ending fun and companionship. Your lust won't be solved by "just doing it this one last time," or watching raunchy shows, pornography, or entertaining sexual intimacy outside of marriage.

Purity For The Mind, Body, And Soul

Your fleshly ailments are solved spiritually. While this may sound cliché, your loneliness is solved by spending more time with God. He is your portion. Psalm 73:26 says, "Though your flesh and heart may fail, GOD is the strength of your heart and your portion, not just for a time, or for a short while, but forever." Your lust isn't solved by giving in because if you do, it will only consume you. The weapons that God has given us have divine power. Divine power destroys strongholds. When we fight with the weapons God has given us, we never lose.

Stop trying to solve flesh problems, with flesh solutions. Solve flesh problems with spiritual solutions.

2 Chronicles 15:7 reminds us that no matter how hard it gets, how weary you get, how difficult it may seem, stay strong. DO NOT GIVE UP. Your work, your tears, your fasting, your praying, and your struggle, they WILL ALL BE REWARDED. All that you're doing now, to separate yourself and walk the way God wants you to walk, it is not in vain. God hears you; He sees you. You may be waiting on your future spouse. You may even be dealing with a difficult spouse or you may be the difficult spouse. You may also be trying to stop having sex, stop watching porn, stop entertaining an ex, or trying to break free from a boyfriend. Whatever it is, God knows! Right now, He's saying, "Please don't give up. Stay strong, your reward is coming. It's on its way."

The devil wants to break you. He doesn't want you to inspire others nor does he want your testimony to encourage the people around you and change lives. He wants to end you quietly and silently, but

I want to inspire you today, your journey isn't just for you. Firsthand blessings are on the way for you, but there are also secondhand blessings. These are the blessings that your family and friends will receive because of your faithfulness. Don't let the devil break you. He'll try and tell you that you've gone too far, and there's no turning back. In those moments, refer to Romans 8:35-39. Will tribulation and all hardships separate us from God? Never! For God, we're being persecuted all day long, and people look at us as weak. But none of this makes us weak. In fact, we are more than victors. We are more than conquerors through Christ! Death, life, angels, demons, rulers, your past, your present, your future, nothing you've done, nothing, nothing, nothing at all, nothing can separate you from God's love. Receive His call and accept His mission for you. Your reward is coming. Hold on, don't give up. God is moving things for your favor, for your deliverance, and for your peace.

Purity For The Mind, Body, And Soul

Our prayer for today is a prayer of thanks, acceptance, and submission. We thank God for being our portion, and our strength when we get weak. We thank Him that no matter what has happened he still is by our side, loving us through our mess. We thank Him for never giving up on us, never taking back His gifts to us, and still leaving us an opportunity to do a great work for Him. We accept the calling He has given to us. We accept the yearning that He's placed on our hearts to let things go, and truly walk with Him in every single aspect of our life. We submit our will, our desires, our fears, our doubts, our pains, our tears, and our weariness. We submit it all to Him today. We leave it all in His hands for Him to handle. We trust that He will work all things together for our good. We ask for Him to continue to lead us, strengthen us, and guide us, so that when the fears, desires, pains and aches return, we take it right back to our Father in heaven. Teach and help us to solve our fleshly problems with spiritual solutions. Anytime we start to rely on our own power, set us straight. We thank You and bless Your holy name for all You've done in our lives, and all You're about to do.

In Jesus' name, Amen.

God Bless.

DAY 15

CLAIM THE VICTORY

1 CORINTHIANS 10:13 ESV

No temptation has overtaken you that is not common to man. God is faithful, and he will not let you be tempted beyond your ability, but with the temptation he will also provide the way of escape, that you may be able to endure it.

You know what purity is.
You know what the problem is.
You know who you are.
You know your triggers.
You know who you're fighting against.
You know you're forgiven.
You know you need to stay on guard.

But do you know you have the victory?

1 Corinthians 10:13 says that your temptations and battles are not uncommon. Anything that God

allows you to be tempted by, it's not beyond your ability to resist. That means any situation that comes your way, through your obedience, you have already won.

Let's break that down. There are situations we put ourselves in, and there are situations that God allows us to go through. If you put yourself in a situation, you have to deal with the consequences. If God tells you not to go to that person's house late at night, and then you go, whatever comes of that situation, whether it be an STD, emotional scarring, etc., that's something you put yourself in. However, if you're minding your business doing and going to where God calls you to, and the option to do wrong comes across your path, God has already given you the strength and will to overcome it and do well. You just have to believe it and walk in it. Let's take Joseph for example. Potiphar's wife was a temptation that came because Joseph was doing what he was supposed to be doing. However, she wasn't beyond his ability to handle. The moment he had a way of escape, he took it. We should follow suit.

Therefore, the first step is to not put yourself in situations you have no business being in. Avoid people, places, and things that aren't going to help you maintain the lifestyle God is calling you to. We established that in the first week. The second step is to walk in victory. Get comfortable with saying no. Get comfortable knowing that any situation, proposition, or temptation that comes your way, God has given you the ability to escape it or overcome it. God is faithful; you will not be tempted past anything you can't overcome. So if a temptation comes and it feels like it's too much, it's actually God telling you, you're capable of far more than you think. You won't be tempted past your endurance; you can bear it. You will always have a way of escape, take it. You are meant to win, every single time. So start living that, walking in that, and believing that.

You're a winner because God said so.

Our prayer today is thanking God for giving us the victory. Ask Him to increase your ability to handle temptation. Ask Him to make escaping temptation become habitual. Pray that we learn from Joseph and do more escaping temptation instead of giving into temptations we already have the victory over. Lastly, ask God to speak to your heart and mind so that you start believing, and living like a champion.

In Jesus' name, Amen.

God Bless.

DAY 16

TERMS OF VICTORY

1 Samuel 15:22 ESV

And Samuel said, "Hath the Lord as great delight in burnt offerings and sacrifices, as in obeying the voice of the Lord? Behold, to obey is better than sacrifice, and to hearken than the fat of rams."
For rebellion is as the sin of witchcraft, and stubbornness is as iniquity and idolatry. Because thou hast rejected the word of the Lord, he hath also rejected thee from being king.

In 1 Samuel 15, we have Saul, the king of Israel, going to war with the Amalekites. God clearly instructs him to wipe everything out and not take anything back. Instead, Saul disobeys and chooses his own terms of victory. As a result, God turns away from him, and rejects Saul as king of Israel.

How often do we do what Saul did? We asked God to expose, separate, and help us overcome the people, and things compromising our purity. God clearly tells us, for example, "This person can't be in your life anymore, or you need to stop watching this show." He clearly details what our terms of victory are. However, after the battle, we suddenly change our terms of victory. Instead of cutting the person off, we don't want to be considered mean or rude, so we decide to just keep them as a friend. Instead of not watching the show, we decide we'll watch but just fast forward through certain scenes. When we do this, we put our victory at jeopardy.

God doesn't need our help or our input to win. He only asks for our complete obedience. However, we as human beings become too occupied about perception. We don't want to be the "bad guy," so we start doing what we think is best, instead of what God said. If God told you, break up with your boyfriend or girlfriend, it's not because He wants to hurt you or them. It's because that's what's best for the both of you. When you obey completely, you reap the blessings of your faithfulness. When you disobey, you have no idea how much more calamity you're bringing into your life.

Remember, God wants what's best for us, so when God is asking you to remove people or things from your life, it's because these things are harmful and will create more hurt, pain, and stress in your life. God is instructing you, not because He wants to control you or make you look bad, but because He wants what's best.

People won't understand and will challenge what God calls you to do. That's ok, follow God's instructions anyway. When we are faithful, even if at the moment it doesn't make sense, or it seems like it's too much, when we look back days, weeks, months, years later, we'll be giving glory to God for what He helped us avoid.

God has already shown you what you have to do and given you clear instructions on exactly how to do it. He has given you the terms of your victory. Follow them precisely, without compromise. Just obey, and trust God. It is better to obey than to give what you think is best. It is better to listen than to do what you think is best.

Our prayer today is to ask God for a heart of complete obedience, to not hesitate or compromise when He asks us to do something, and to do exactly as He asks of us. Help us learn not to try and fix His plan or His instructions. Help us to trust God completely and just listen. Help us to just trust and obey.

In Jesus' name, Amen.

God Bless.

DAY 17

GIVE THANKS

LUKE 17: 15-19 NIV

One of them, when he saw he was healed, came back, praising God in a loud voice. He threw himself at Jesus' feet and thanked him— and he was a Samaritan. Jesus asked, "Were not all ten cleansed? Where are the other nine? Has no one returned to give praise to God except this foreigner?" Then he said to him, "Rise and go; your faith has made you well."

Sometimes during fasts and prayers, we get focused on fervently asking God for things we may forget to thank Him for coming through for us. My hope is that God has done some amazing things for you during these last few weeks. There's been battles, there's been victories, mindsets have been shifted. Things that were obstacles in your walk have been removed, and clarity and communication between you and God should be better than ever before.

In the midst of God shifting things inside you and also in your life, let's just take time out to give Him thanks.

Thanks for the creation of the fast and your participation. Thanks for the revelations He's given you.

Thanks for exposing the things in your life that are hindering your walk with God. Thanks for exposing the things and/or people that are compromising your purity. Thanks for the courage and strength to make real changes in your life that lead you closer to Christ-like character.

When Jesus healed the 10 lepers, only one of them had the presence of mind to go back to Him and say thank you. Let's not be the majority and forget to give thanks. There are things God has separated you from these past weeks that were in your life to create a lot of pain, hurt, and dysfunction. He's protecting you from weapons seen and unseen. If that doesn't deserve a praise and a mighty thanks, then I don't know what does.

1 THESSALONIANS 5:16-18 ESV

Rejoice always, pray continually, give thanks in all circumstances; for this is God's will for you in Christ Jesus.

As we pray today, I just want us to give thanks to God for what He's been doing for you during this fast, and what He will be doing for you even after.

In Jesus' name, Amen.

God Bless.

DAY 18

SHARE YOUR TESTIMONY

MARK 5:19 ESV

And he did not permit him but said to him, "Go home to your friends and tell them how much the Lord has done for you, and how he has had mercy on you."

GALATIANS 6:2 ESV

Bear one another's burdens, and so fulfill the law of Christ.

Throughout this fast, I pray it has been a transformative experience. I pray that each day has drawn you closer to God and the lifestyle He's calling you to. I pray you're now able to see things in a way you haven't been able to before, that your discernment is stronger than ever, and your prayer life is even more consistent. However, now that you have been able to benefit, the next step is to share your testimony with whomever God leads you to.

God's love is not meant to be given and simply

kept. The Bible says that God's love is made complete when we love others. He loves us. We love Him, and then we love others. Mark 5:19 says that we should tell our friends and family what God has done for us and how He's given us grace and mercy. The people in our lives need to know that God is still doing amazing things in people's lives. In the world we live in today, purity is an after-thought. It's considered something that isn't realistic or isn't feasible. However, God is calling those who are willing to stand for Him to show the world that Christ-like purity does exist, to show that your bodies were made to honor God, not satisfy lust; to show that your bodies are not your own, they are vessels, a temple to be used by God.

Your testimony matters. It may be as big as a sermon in front of a congregation, or maybe as intimate as a one-on-one conversation with a friend. Allow God to decide where and to whom you are to share your experience but don't keep the blessings and the change you've experienced a secret. There are millions of people searching for what God has given you.

Galatians 6:2 says, "Bear one another's burdens, and so fulfill the law of Christ."

God has given you the victory not so you can gloat, but so you can be an example and inspiration to others. Help your fellow brothers and sisters in Christ, so they too may overcome and find victory in their own battles.

Purity For The Mind, Body, And Soul

Our prayer today is that You, God, grant us the courage to share our testimony, the discernment to know who we should share our experience with, and for our lives to be a blessing to the people around us. We pray that our words and our lives be aligned with Your will for us. We rebuke any spirit of fear, hesitance, and intimidation. Help us walk boldly for You.

In Jesus' name, Amen.

God Bless.

Feel free to share your experience so far and what the fast has done in your life up to this point!! You can share publicly, or share privately!

DAY 19

IT'S NOT JUST ABOUT YOU

MATTHEW 5:16 ESV

In the same way, let your light shine before others, so that they may see your good works and give glory to your Father who is in heaven.

As we are nearing the end of the fast, there is something I want to stress to you. It's about us, but it's also about far more than us. God loves you more than you could ever know, but He loves everyone else just as much. Just as He has plans for you, He also has plans for your friends, family, and even your enemies. Your commitment to purity is not something that will only affect you. Its impact will go farther than you can imagine.

Let's take for example Michelle Obama. This is a wonderful woman who has impacted countless lives. Being First Lady definitely heightened her profile, especially with how she handled the love and adoration, but also the hate and criticism. She has set standards for character that resonate with people and is a much-needed role model for black women. Now, imagine if Barack Obama's mother chose not to have him. If Barack was never born, Michelle Obama wouldn't have become the woman we know her to be today. We know her as the wife of Barack Obama, the first black president of the United States. This is not to say she wouldn't have married another future black president nor is her impact and greatness diminished. However, all other scenarios are just hypotheticals and empty arguments. Who we do know her as is who she is today, and Barack's mother had decisions that could have reshaped the world as we know it today.

That's the magnitude in which God is trying to reveal to you. Your decisions hold far more impact than you realize. Your commitment to purity could lead you to start practicing celibacy, which now helps you avoid an STI that you would have received had you kept having sex. Your commitment to purity could stop you from trying to court your future spouse's best friend, ensuring that you don't ruin the potential to be together.

God doesn't think small. His ways are not our ways. His thoughts are not our thoughts. He's calling you because He has amazing things in store for you. However, it doesn't only impact you. You are the light of the world. That means people who have never seen light will have a chance to because of your decisions and your impact.

At first this fast wasn't something I wanted to write. With all the things I have going on in my life, I could have easily passed on this. Yet, the moment I decided to be obedient, I was able to see how God was using my obedience to be a blessing to others, and there's far more impact than I'm even aware of. It's not just about us. Blessings reverberate.

So as Matthew 5:16 says, "Let's be a light before others." Why? Because they need to see what light looks like. They need to see examples of Christians who aren't afraid to pursue purity. They need to see singles who are waiting on God and marriages without infidelity. The world sees enough destruction and dysfunction. They need to see examples of what God is calling them to. Why do they need to see it? It will cause them to have hope. They will be able to see what happens if they too surrender to God; He will do the same, if not, more in their lives. Why does all this need to happen? All for God's glory.

It's not just about you. It's not just about them. It's all about God.

Our prayer today is that God keeps us humble, to help us understand that the work He is doing in us isn't only for us. We pray that we are being turned into lighthouses for His glory and living testimonies to bring others to Him. Help us not to get self-centered and become focused on what only benefits us. Help us to accept that there is a much bigger picture we can't even begin to fathom. Let our actions not only bring blessings to us but also blessings to those around us. Let us be that light for Christ at all times.

In Jesus' name, Amen.

God Bless.

DAY 20
PRACTICE WHAT GOD TEACHES

GALATIANS 6:7- 9 ESV

Do not be deceived: God is not mocked, for whatever one sows, that will he also reap. For the one who sows to his own flesh will from the flesh reap corruption, but the one who sows to the Spirit will from the Spirit reap eternal life. And let us not grow weary of doing good, for in due season we will reap, if we do not give up.

PHILIPPIANS 1:6 ESV

And I am sure of this, that he who began a good work in you will bring it to completion at the day of Jesus Christ.

This is not the end. This is the beginning. God didn't have you enter this fast just so you could "behave" for 21 days and then go back to life as usual right after. There's been a shift. Through prayer and this fast, you have been sowing spiritual seeds. These seeds are going to bear fruit, if they haven't already. You will have new friendships, new relationships, new mindsets, and new standards. God is taking you into a new season of your life because you were willing to be obedient. You sacrificed and resisted your flesh, and God honors sacrifice.

Galatians 6:7-9 says, "God can't be fooled. Whatever you put your time and energy into, intentionally or unintentionally, you will deal with the consequences." You see, the word consequence tends to have a negative connotation, but it's defined as a result or effect of an action. So consequences are neither good or bad, they're just results. To bring it all together, if as a young man you spent your entire youth chasing female after female, you are sowing a seed. Don't be surprised if as soon as you get married, you still revert back to that same behavior. That's where you sowed your seeds; that is the fruit you bear. In the same light, we have the young lady who never allowed herself to be swayed by any man. It won't be any surprise that she maintains that same behavior during her marriage, why? Because that's what she practiced. That's the seeds she sowed.

God has made it clear to you, if you keep submitting to your flesh, to your urges, your carnal desires, it will do nothing but reap corruption. It will corrupt your relationships, your friendships, your work, your ministry, and even your mind. How often do we hear about ministers whose lives are destroyed because they couldn't control their lust? Let us not judge them, but let us learn from them so that we don't make similar mistakes.

Sow your seeds in the spirit, and you will reap blessings upon blessings. God clearly says it, "Sow to the spirit, and you will reap eternal life. Seek ye first the kingdom of God, and all these things shall be added unto you." There are blessings in obedience to God.

We know obedience can get hard, tiring, frustrating, and feel at times even impossible. However, God says, do not grow weary in well doing. Don't give in, just keep at it. Why? Why not just do whatever you want and release the tension? Why should I keep at this whole purity thing? Because if you continue, you will reap the rewards in due season. Your season is coming. Your time is closer than you think. Don't give up. The fast was to boost and lift you up. It is your second wind. Keep sowing, the harvest is coming. When the fast is over, let your prayer life get stronger, let your purity get firmer, become even more on fire for God. If you're reading this, it's because God has something prepared for you, but your purity needs to be in check. You will reap in due season if you don't give up. God started a work in you, and He won't stop until it's completed. Don't give up.

We're just getting started.

Our prayer for today is to ask God to fire us up even more when the fast is over. We pray for God to let this be the beginning of real transformation and change in our lives, to help us continue pursuing purity, and growth. We pray for God to reveal to us other aspects of our lives that may be found lacking, even if just a little. We pray that He help us dig into scripture more, to use and apply them in our everyday challenges. We thank God for what He's doing and what He will continue doing. We ask that God just help us hold on until Christ returns.

In Jesus' name, Amen.

God Bless.

DAY 21

PURELY THE POINT

Ephesians 2:8-9 NKJV

For by grace you have been saved through faith, and that not of yourselves; it is the gift of God, not of works, lest anyone should boast.

Acts 16:30-31 NKJV

"Sirs, what must I do to be saved?" So they said, "Believe on the Lord Jesus Christ, and you will be saved, you and your household."

Romans 10:9-10 ESV

"That if you confess with your mouth, 'Jesus is Lord,' and believe in your heart that God raised him from the dead, you will be saved. For it is with your heart that you believe and are justified, and it is with your mouth that you confess and are saved."

During this purity fast, we've covered a lot. We have defined purity, identified different aspects of it, identified ways to fight back, ways to gain the victory, and so on and so forth. However, there is an important point I want to stress. Purity doesn't save you. It doesn't earn you salvation nor does it make you "better" than anyone else. We pursue purity because that's what God calls us to, not because it helps us earn our way into the Kingdom. We pursue purity because that's his will for our lives, not the consequences that come with stepping outside His will. We pursue purity because that's undeniably what is best for us. Purity is important, but it's not our means of salvation. Salvation is by grace and acceptance of Christ. Ephesians 2:8-9 says, "We have been saved by grace through our faith, through our belief. It was God's gift to us, not something we earned." So as you go on this journey, don't get caught in the mindset that the more pure you are, the more God loves you, or if you slip, your salvation is at stake. God loves us unconditionally. Our obedience to His will is so we can reap the blessings, so we can share our testimony and help others, and so we can avoid the consequences that come when we ignore God's warnings.

If purity doesn't lead to my salvation, what must I do to be saved? Well, Acts 16:30-31 answers that. It says you must believe on the Lord Jesus Christ. Romans 10: 9-10 says, "You must confess Jesus is Lord with your mouth, and you believe that Christ is God's Son and that he rose from the dead." Your belief in Christ justifies you, and your confession saves you.

When you truly believe in something, it affects how you act. If you believe you can trust someone, you share secrets and take chances on them that you wouldn't normally take with anyone else. In that same light, because we believe in Christ, we believe in His word. His word tells us to flee youthful passions, to stay away from sexual immorality, to think about things that are good, pure, and righteous. That's why we pursue it, not because it will secure salvation, but because it allows God to move even more in our life through our obedience.

When you commit to purity, it isn't because you want to be saved, it's because you want to be faithful to God in that aspect of your life, and rightly so. The blessings and benefits you will reap because of it are invaluable and incalculable. You reap what you sow.

Let us step forward today, inviting God into every aspect of our lives. Purity was the start for some, maybe the middle, and maybe even the final stronghold for others. Regardless of where you are in your Christian journey, just keep walking. Let's keep running our race and helping our fellow brothers and sisters. Let's encourage them so that we become a community of believers, not only believing in Christ, but living like Christ.

This has been an amazing 21 days, and I pray God blesses your sacrifice and your commitment. Keep your eyes focused on Christ, and let Him be your guiding light, forever and always.

Our final prayer is that we thank God for making it through, that He take full control of our lives and continue to reveal to us any aspects of our lives that aren't aligned with His will. We pray that we stay focused on the main goal, which is to be saved. We ask God to bless the seeds we have been sowing these past 3 weeks and that He direct our path in all things. We thank God for leading us to adapt a lifestyle of purity and becoming more Christ-like. We pray that when our race is done, He'll look upon us and say, "Well done, my good and faithful servant."

In Jesus' name, Amen.

God Bless.

ABOUT THE AUTHOR

Assel Jean-Pierre Jr is a Haitian American, New York native, who is a speaker, professional pianist, producer, and author. He is married to the beautiful Genevieve Jean-Pierre, and the father of his baby boy, Saphir Jean-Pierre. He is also a choir director that uses his God-given talents to better his church community, all to God's glory. Assel also is an audio engineer, and songwriter for JPSonic Studios. He has two albums, Hymns of Meditation for the Soul Vol. 1 and Vol. 2, by the Jean-Pierre Pianists. He is currently working on various projects with multiple artists. He is also the producer of the live performance, The Jean-Pierre Pianists Show. His goals are to do whatever God calls him to do at the highest level. He desires to make the most out of his God-given talent and hard work, but most importantly, to follow wherever God leads him.

CONNECT WITH THE AUTHOR

Email: **Selzjpinc@gmail.com**
Follow him on Instagram: **@Selzjp**
Connect with him on Facebook:
Assel Jean-Pierre Jr

www.ingramcontent.com/pod-product-compliance
Lightning Source LLC
Chambersburg PA
CBHW060032040426
42333CB00042B/2399